AF271101

Whispers
in the Dark

By Dr. Terri Lane Hunt

Chosen Pen Publishing

Whispers in the Dark/Dr. Terri Lane Hunt
ISBN 978-1-952315-91-6
Paperback

To order additional copies of the resource, write Chosen Pen Customer Service: 1420 Hoke Loop Road Fayetteville, NC 28314 Fax orders to 910-868-3300 Phone orders to 910-818-6652

Website:

www.chosepen.com
www.chosenpenacademy.com

Library of Congress Control Number: 2024919130

Unless otherwise noted all scriptures are from the King James Version Bible.

Printed in the United States of America

Table of Contents

Acknowledgments

To my Father and Sister, Frank Jackson Sr., and Mary Ann Jackson, as well as my Best Friend, Linda Fleming, You are gone but never forgotten.

To my Mother, Adeline Scott Jackson, and my Sisters, Loretta Bush, Catherine Jackson Tillery, Wendy Jackson Livous, and Velma Marline Jackson.

To my gifts from God, my two Daughters, Seneca Robertson (Shun), and Crystal Harris (Preston).

To my five Grandchildren, DeErika Jones, Cristian Harris, Preston Harris Jr., Jaziya Sumlin, Kristopher Sumlin.

To my best Girlfriends, you know who you are, I love you all.

To my "ride or die" friend, I call my "TIGER," the Author, Alton Jones Jr.

To my New Direction Christian Church family, and especially my Golden Seniors Connect Group.

I thank you all for not only embracing my journey but also embarking on your own. I thank you all for sharing my experience with cancer with empathy and accepting my lessons with love.

"Always remember that
healing, happiness, and wholeness
are developed by returning
to stillness within your most authentic self."
                                    -Dr. Terri Lane Hunt

Foreword

The purpose of a "foreword" is to move the reader forward and prepare them for what the author has so skillfully and openly decided to share with the world.

Dr. Terri Lane Hunt's life in print is a testimony to the power of determination, persistence, and a heart for God to bring hope and healing. I have known Terri for many years as a teacher and a friend, and I knew the first time she hugged me that I was loved.

I knew when I talked with her that I was being fully heard. And, I knew when she talked that I was the recipient of a gift that everyone should experience. Through this book, Terri has found a way to offer her gifts to the world. Everywhere Terri goes, the people she encounters know they have met a lady who is full of love for God's people.

This book will serve as a guide to help others who are searching for understanding of their path in life and God's plan and how it all serves God's purpose. **Jeremiah 29:11** says, *"For I know the plans I have for you, declares the Lord. Plans to prosper you and not to harm you, plans to give you hope and a future."* As you move forward to read Terri's story, know that where there is hope, there can be healing.

Susan C. Brooks
Friend and Fellow Educator

Dr. Terri Lane Hunt

"Thanks be to God for His Transforming Work!!"

-excerpt from Dr. Floyd Covey's Preface

Preface

Over the past four decades, God has given me the privilege of journeying with countless people as a Spiritual Director, Wisdom and Soul Guide, and Psychologist. It is such a joy for me as I observe many of those individuals come to know God more intimately and to understand themselves more fully. It has been a special joy for me to journey with Dr. Terri Lane Hunt and to watch her transformation take place.

She has courageously faced past wounds and hurts and allowed the healing power of Christ Jesus to flow through her being. Dr. Hunt has fulfilled a calling and dream in the writing of this book, "Whispering in the Dark." She has been quite transparent in the telling of her story and her reflection on the healing work which God has done and is doing in her life. This book and its accompanying journal have the potential of being helpful to those persons who are seeking healing and transformation in their lives. For each of us, it is essential that we journey inward to begin the healing process.

There, we can allow the Holy Spirit to guide us to explore our lifetime of hurts and wounds. Only then can we begin the process of moving outward into our relationships with other people. I no longer believe in the concept of change.

That is to say, I no longer believe that it is possible for us to make and maintain changes in our lives, in and of ourselves, without the active presence of God. You may think that it is possible to change. However, consider the millions of people who make New Year's resolutions: to eat healthier; to work out more; to go to church more often; to spend more time with the family, etc. How long do those behavioral changes typically last?

Perhaps a few weeks, and then we return to our former behaviors. There are usually at least two reasons why changes don't last. First, our behaviors are generally the result of our thoughts and beliefs: i.e., in other words, our interior life. Our behaviors are symptoms, rather than the actual issue. Thus, behaviors do not change without our first undergoing transformation in our interior life. The second reason, and the more important one, is that change is not actually a Biblical concept.

If we were capable of changing ourselves, the Incarnation of Jesus may have been unnecessary. A few years ago, the Holy Spirit led me to two passages of Holy Scripture.

In St. Paul's letter to the Romans, we read: *"Don't copy the behaviors and customs of this world. Instead, let God transform you into a new person."* **(Romans 12:2 NLT).**

In St. Paul's second letter to the Corinthians, we read: *"This means that anyone who belongs to Christ has become a new person. The old life has gone; a new life has begun! All of this is a gift from God, who brought us back to Himself through Christ."* **(II Corinthians 5:17-18a).**

In the light of these Scriptures, our task is as follows: We need to pray that God will enable us to surrender ourselves to Him and to His Love so that He can transform us into who He created us to be. Thus, we look to God to transform us internally, instead of attempting to change our behaviors ourselves.

Thanks be to God for His transforming work!! This transformation approach is the one which Dr. Hunt has taken in her own life, as well as in the writing of this book, 'Whispering in the Dark."

This transformation takes place only when both God and self are deeply known. Dr. Hunt's book outlines her own healing process as she has learned to surrender herself to God's loving presence. As you read this book, you may become aware of some of the wounds of your own life journey.

• • •

If this happens for you, I strongly encourage you to contact your Pastor, a counselor, or other licensed professional to assist you on your journey. We do not need to journey alone.

Obviously, continue to pray to God and to seek His guidance for your life. May you be filled with the Grace, Peace, Love, Joy, Hope, and Mercy of the Blessed Holy Trinity!!

Dr. Floyd Covey

Written, under the inspiration of the Holy Spirit, on this Holy Day of St. Zaccheus of Jerusalem, by Dr. Floyd L. Covey, Sr., D.D.; Th.D.; Ph.D.; C. Carm. of C.T.P.; O.SS.T. Bishop / Priest / Psychologist / Monk / Spiritual Director / Wisdom Guide

www.drfloydcovey.com

"This journey has been about finding peace, the peace necessary for me to bloom boldly, intentionally, and unapologetically."

-Dr. Terri Lane Hunt

Introduction

There is a season in life when we encounter pain that will stop us all in our tracks. For some, the pain will shake them to the core. It will have you questioning your life. What you thought to be true will be revealed as false. Who you thought to be in your corner to trust, will be revealed as those who perpetrated or orchestrated your pain or trauma. In contrast, those you would consider as perfect strangers will become your champions and cheerleaders, those who serve to assist you in understanding the facades of life and overcoming everything behind your every pain.

After decades of holding onto the pains of life, I decided that now was the time for honesty with myself and to do what was necessary to heal. This journey not only required honesty, but it also required full transparency. Now was the time to get real with myself and my situation if I wanted to move forward. I knew that revisiting the past would require a deep dive. It would require that I relive the pain and the pressure, and in doing so, I would better understand the purpose of it all. The last three years of complete authenticity have been very painful but powerful. It was excruciating but enlightening. And while I have felt that it was destructive at times, I know that it has been critical for my growth and development.

This journey was a personal one. It has been strictly about my healing, and understanding the root of my emotional, spiritual, and personal truth. This journey has been about pruning away that which does not serve me - dead mindsets, relationships, and environments.

This journey has been about finding peace, the peace necessary for me to bloom boldly, intentionally, and unapologetically. This journey has been about the lessons learned and the maturity required to become the better version of myself.

There was once a time when my perspective concerning my life, and my experiences resulted in nothing but tear-stained pillows. I lived my life from the only thing that I could see and feel, and that was pain. The pain of discomfort, disappointment, and disdain mixed with the pain of loss, grief, and anger, felt like a never-ending journey of destruction and depression. All I could see was heartache because my heart had been shattered time after time.

Once I decided to see things for what they were, a veil was lifted. I began to see the world, my family, so-called friends, and even myself and my life as it was and not as I thought it to be. The reality of it all began to set in and what happened next didn't feel good, but it was very necessary.

I found myself detaching myself from the people I thought I wanted in my life forever. I began to see my flaws and the issues that came from not correcting them, and I began to seek God more than I ever had. I lost loved ones. I lost my way and most of all, I lost myself. I was so drained, depressed, and depleted, but my Father God picked up my broken pieces and developed my faith and character. He showed me the purpose of the experiences. The insecurities and negative emotions that were intended to break me, were used to build up my faith and bolstered my efforts to find myself and a greater purpose for my life as a person and as a Christian.

I have cried more in this season than I have ever cried in my entire life. In the same breath, I also acknowledge that I have learned and grown more than I have cried.

As time passed, self-work ensued. A greater understanding of what spiritual warfare looks like resulted in a better life and a better understanding of purpose. I went from tears of grief to tears of growth and tears of joy. Everything began to make sense.

My tears had a purpose. They were there to teach me, awaken my spirit, and truly open my eyes. Every test, whether I initially passed or failed, taught me, and served to help me mature in every way possible. I now know that my tears were more than proof of my pain. They were a testament to my conviction and an integral part of my pruning process. They are now a symbol of my joy and freedom.

Every trial, test, triumph, and pain taught me to acknowledge Father God. The water that the enemy thought would drown me, God used to baptize me and clean me up. Because of the tears, I learned to whisper my every concern to God in prayer.

As I share my journey within the pages of this book, you will better understand how all areas of my life were affected by pain. Most importantly, you will better understand how I survived it all and how my "Whispers in the Dark" were key to my overcoming. My prayer is that after reading this book you will never feel bad about shedding tears. Your tears are also whispered prayers to our Father.

Dr. Terri Lane Hunt

Author

"Don't copy the behaviors and customs of this world. Instead, let God transform you into a new person."
(Romans 12:2 NLT)

I Don't Know Prayer

(Author Unknown)

You just go somewhere quiet and
you sit at the feet of God and you say, ***"I don't know."***
I don't know where to go from here.
I don't know what is happening.
I don't know how to process this.
I don't know what to do with these emotions.
I don't know how to handle this situation.
And then with whatever little grain of faith you have to say,
"but you know."
And you leave it there. God most certainly hears your
prayer.
Amen if you trust God.

"For I know the plans I have for you, declares the Lord.
Plans to prosper you and not to harm you,
plans to give you hope and a future."
Jeremiah 29:11

Chapter One

Who is God to Me?

Depending upon where you are from and who you ask, the definition of who God is may vary. Some equate Him to the things we see in nature. Others may share their understanding of Him as the person described by a relative or friend. There is even a community of people that deny His existence altogether. My response is much more personal because God is my everything.

In child-like wonder, I had varied perspectives of God and how He is represented in my life and the lives of others. Much of what I knew or understood came from the stories told by others. I came to know God as my ***provider, my healer, and my problem solver***. When I heard people at church say that God was a provider, I understood just how He provided for me and my family, because our family had what most in our neighborhood could only dream about. God made it possible for us to have more than enough to give others and for that reason, I was thankful.

One of the biggest lessons that my mother taught us was to give to others. Every summer we were able to share experiences with our friends because my parents would rent a bus to take us to Six Flags over Texas. My siblings and I could invite six friends and altogether we stayed the weekend and had fun. This was just one example of how my parents' showed generosity and instilled in us the importance of being a blessing to others. They often expressed that we should show love to each other and those around us. Taking our friends on trips and feeding others in the community was how they showed love.

As a small child, I learned that God was a healer. He healed me as a young child from bleeding ulcers. And, when my father had a massive heart attack when I was about 16 years old, I prayed that God would heal him. God did just that.

During the years I faced an abuser, I often wondered to myself, *"Where is the God that was supposed to make everything all right?"* My prayers to Him seemed to go unanswered and while I was taught that I could trust Him, I could not understand His apparent absence during my time of abuse. He was supposed to be a problem solver, but my problem never seemed to go away. Looking back, I now know that God was my rescuer. He freed me from this very detrimental situation.

What began as a child of 9 years old until about the age of 16 years old, may have had me questioning his presence and His timing, but I now know through all my life experiences, that He was always there. His responses to my questions and my cries were always right on time. He is faithful as promised, and His Word is one thing I learned that I could depend on. He and His Word are one and what he promises us, He delivers.

For I am convinced that neither death nor life, neither angels, nor demons, neither the present nor the future, nor any powers, neither height nor depth, nor anything else in all creation, will be able to separate us from the love of God that is in Christ Jesus our Lord.

Romans 8:38-39

Chapter Two

When the Whispers Began

Most simplistically, "whispers in the dark" are those times in which I had private conversations with God. They were always at night, under my covers, and after I would have secured my doorway with towels to make sure I could drown out all sounds. In addition, I didn't want anyone to hear what I shared with God during whispering moments.

Like many growing up in the South, we attended church regularly. Attending weekly services and serving in the church was a way of life. It was during this time that I heard about God. In addition to this, I was taught all the bible stories from our neighbor, Reverend Phillip. He made the stories interesting and vivid to the imagination. In addition to the stories, he told me about the times to come. The times we are living in now. Reverend Phillip made a big impression on me when it came to understanding the Word of God. His stories opened the door and introduced me to God.

When I look back on my childhood, I grew up quickly. When I should have been engaging in youthful activities, I was home-bound, cooking, cleaning, doing homework, preparing for school, and caring for my younger siblings. While my friends at school or in the neighborhood would be enjoying the freedoms of youthfulness, I served as a watch guard for my younger sisters. It was a duty I knew that I was required to take on. I could not allow what had been happening to me, to happen to them. What started around age 9 continued until I left for college and my mother didn't seem to mind. When she and my father went away for the weekends, having me in charge of things was no problem. It was something I had been doing anyway. When my sisters had a need or concern, they often came to me before going to our mother.

As a teen, I realized I needed God in my life. I needed Him to help me throughout my Junior High and High School years. By this time, I could feel things changing for me and the demands were beginning to weigh heavy. In addition to all that I was doing within our household, I became concerned about things that most teenagers find themselves concerned about. I didn't want anything to develop into an issue with my parents and I didn't want any additional stress. God was my answer, or at least that is what I had heard others say at church.

So, I added more to discuss with him during my whispering moments. I needed Him to help me overcome my first boy crush. When I didn't study for a test and needed to pass, I didn't hesitate to call on Him. Again, I did not want to get in trouble with my parents. My parents were big on education. My Father, who never graduated beyond the 7th grade, encouraged education. He wanted us to do well and to gain as much as we could. He reminded us that God granted him favor to have the job that he had, and it was by God's grace that he had a home for us as well. I took all that he shared with us to heart. It served as the motivation to always excel and to never settle for average. I hope that I have made him proud.

During my teen years, I began to suffer from bleeding ulcers. The older I got, the worse the condition became for me. I eventually learned that the ulcers came from worry and stress brought on by my years of victimization, no doubt. From the age of 9 years old, I was sexually assaulted by a relative who not only took my innocence but would often remind me that if I told anyone he would kill me. I lived in a state of constant fear and torment.

The first occurrence with this family member, one that I should have been able to trust, was at my family's home, a place that should have been considered my haven. I can remember my first incident like it was yesterday. My sisters and I were playing with our paper dolls on the front porch. He called me and asked me to bring him some water, to which I responded accordingly. After giving him the water, he cornered me in the kitchen. He told me that he had something for me, but I could not tell anyone about it. As any child would be, I was curious.

I thought he had a gift or candy to give me. In his next breath, he threatened me saying that he would kill me if I shared what was about to happen. Before I could make sense of his statement, he began touching me in areas that should have been off-limits. I didn't know what to do. I was paralyzed. I was afraid. I felt vulnerable and very much alone. There were so many emotions flooding my mind that I became lightheaded and felt as if I were about to pass out. As soon as I could get away from him, I ran to my bedroom, closed the door, got in bed, and began to cry. I stayed in my room for the remainder of the day rest of the summer.

I was traumatized as you can imagine. The experience was not only disturbing but it caused me to suffer continued emotional, physical, and psychological trauma for years to come. I wish that I could say that this was the first and only incident, but the abuse by this family member, who was given free rein in our home by my parents, continued for years. And, just like the first time, I always felt afraid, became paralyzed, and alone. I felt nasty. I felt like isolation was the best way to deal with this; however, it was during my times of isolation that my mind would wander. The isolation eventually led to me suffering from panic attacks and ultimately being diagnosed with bleeding ulcers. This was the beginning of my journey of seeing God as my closest confidant.

For He shall give His angels charge over you,
to keep you in all your ways.
Psalm 91:11

Chapter Three

My Guardian Angel, Nurse Mary

One of the best things that could have been given to me as a young girl was my relationship with God. I knew Him, feared Him, and worshipped Him. Despite all that I was experiencing as a child, I found solace in connecting with God. As horrible as the circumstances were, I knew that my whispering to Him was effective, somehow.

As already shared, I suffered from ulcers. My parents and my doctor, Dr. Brooks, knew about the ulcers and how bad they were in my stomach. I had great parents, and I knew that they trusted Dr. Brooks, but no one ever asked the question that needed to be asked. Nobody, at any time, asked me, "What is troubling you? What is making you sick?" Each visit brought its own measure of trauma. My dietary restrictions meant eating nothing because my stomach burned. Every 3 to 4 months meant hospitalization and drinking a nasty white chalky substance. My menstrual cycles were horrible and every time (my offender) visited; I could feel the ulcers eating more at the lining in my stomach.

One day while in the hospital, I heard the doctor say to my parents that if my ulcers didn't heal, I may not be able to have children. "The ulcers would "eat up" anything living in her stomach," the doctor said. Hearing this had me feeling as if I had been hit with a ton of bricks. I thought, *"Me! Terri Jackson will not have children. The devil is a lie!"* I wanted to be someone's mother. I wanted four children, two boys, and two girls.

Inevitably, I later required hospitalization again. At this point, I lost count as to how many times I had to be admitted. During the night, the reoccurring comments in my head from the doctor kept me crying for days. The crying only led to more bleeding and more pain in my stomach. That was until Mary, the night nurse, came into my room. I thought her visit would be like any other nurse; taking my blood and checking vitals. Upon her entering my room, I was crying profusely under the covers. She pulled back my covers and asked why was I so sad. As I looked at her, tears still flowing, I shared with her all that I heard the doctor share with my parents and my desire to be a mother one day. Mary listened and then hugged me. This hug and interaction were like no other.

When I reflect on this visit with Mary, I can recall that her white uniform was whiter than anything I had ever seen. Her complexion was a pinkish tone. She didn't appear to be a white woman, and I knew that she wasn't Black, but she was very caring. Her voice was soft and calming. The touch of her hand was soft like cotton and when she embraced me, to calm my spirits, I felt a rush throughout my body that can only described as soothing heat. It rushed from the crown of my head to the sole of my feet.

After the hug, she asked me if I attended church. My reply was, "yes." I told her that I loved attending church and that I loved God. She then told me that God could fix my situation. She added that God could heal my body and that there was nothing too hard for Him. I listened intently but then replied that I was just a teenager and God would not listen to me. So, I suggested my dad pray for me. She then gave me the best advice ever. She told me God wanted to hear from my heart and encouraged me to talk with Him like I was talking with her. She further added that fancy words were not required, only speak from my heart.

Upon departure from my room, Mary reassured me that God was waiting to hear from me. She called me precious as she prepared to leave my room. I asked her if she would come by for a visit the next day. She told me that she sees me always then smiled and walked out the door.

• • •

I asked for Mary the next 3 days while at the hospital. Nobody knew of Mary who worked the night shift. After asking so many times an older woman, a black nurse, told me that Nurse Mary did not work the night that I referenced. I was told that another nurse was on duty that evening. That made no sense to me because Mary hugged me, and her hug was different, and our conversation was real. It was then that the nurse added, Mary was your guardian angel sent from heaven. That was the day I started believing in angels. That was the night I was healed of my ulcers.

"Anyone who believes in Him will never be put to shame."
Romans 10:11

Chapter Four

Trying to Understand Pain

Unlike young girls my age, I never dated in high school. I am sure the opportunity would have been there to date, but because I did not trust people, considering my trauma I wanted to protect myself sexually; I avoided it. As I approached graduation, I wanted to attend my prom. It was going to serve as my official declaration of adulthood and moving forward. My best friend's brother was to be my date. We all had grown up together and I trusted him. Prom was going to be my new beginning.

My mother took me shopping at an upscale boutique named Poison Ivy. I chose an off-white jumpsuit, with fringes from one sleeve to another. My shoes, more of a bootie, matched perfectly with the ensemble. I was going to be sharp and turn heads that night. Unfortunately, my prom plans were short-lived.

A few days before prom, my mother received a call from a family member alleging that I had been promiscuous with Caucasian boys at school. This family member, only two years older than me, also attended school with me. She, unlike myself, was the flirt and the boy she had her eye on was not the least bit interested. He was my classmate and a friend, but not someone who I dated or was even interested in dating. The truth of the matter is that the family member disliked my friendship with him and because he was not welcoming of her advances, she lied to my mother. That lie resulted in me missing my prom. This family member, on my mother's side of the family, was the cause of me missing the biggest event of my life. Just like the male cousin who had been violating me, I had been violated again and put on punishment because of jealousy and lies. Even today, the thought of this betrayal from family cuts like a knife. As they often say, it is those who are closest to you that hurt you the most.

I was so unhappy as a teenager, but I knew how to pray, and I knew how to trust and believe in God. I had seen his hands in and on my life, all my life. I felt Him in my heart because I loved His people. I felt him because I could forgive the worst of people and the things they had done to me. Knowing and fearing God at an early age is one of my biggest accomplishments.

As a teen, I often asked God why so much pain. God said those are growing pains and these are purpose pains, the pains that bring you into your purpose. Sometimes pain moves you to another level. When you become uncomfortable, you move and that move leads you to the next level. Pain can be your test to a new beginning. Sometimes people cause you pain because you will never let go or move on, and God allows them to hurt you so you can let it go. Remember your first love? That heartbreak was like "I am going to die" – this is too much to manage. My heart is going to burst open. Lord help me! There is no medicine for heartache. Only time that seems so far away. The best part is that we got over it. God carried us when we could not carry ourselves, even when we thought the pain was unbearable.

At the age of 17, my parents gave me a graduation gift like none other. While my father wasn't as excited as my mom, I was ready for this trip of a lifetime. Going to another country would be an adventure as well as an escape from what I had been facing for years at the hands of the family pedophile. Looking back, this trip could have been my mother's way of making up for me missing prom. Regardless of the reason why, I was excited.

My first stop was the home of my uncle in Karlsruhe, Germany. I stayed with his family for three weeks. He was a soldier and eventually returned to the United States. After his departure, I lived with an aunt whose husband was in the military as well. They were stationed at Pirmasens, Germany. I lived with them for 3 weeks as well.

I loved my six-week stay in Germany. My first impression of the county was that it was the most beautiful and the cleanest place ever. I grew to love the culture and the food. Eating lobster became one of my favorite things to do. Being away was a gift that made the biggest impact not simply because of what I experienced, but because it also placed me in a safe place and allowed me to experience things I had never imagined.

One of the best memories of living in Germany is the friendship gained with Lavern. She was the first stranger to welcome me to the country. Her home was military housing and she was the neighbor to my aunt. She and her husband had an adorable son. To see how she interacted with her son was beautiful. In some way, it made me a little jealous. She was gentle, caring, and very protective of her child. I wished that I could have felt the same way about the care that I received from my parents. Don't get me wrong, my mother and father did their best, but Lavern's care was far beyond what I had ever seen.

Because of the generosity and hospitality of my aunt and Uncle, I grew as a person. The experience of Germany, allowed me to see life differently and to realize that there was more to life than what I had been exposed to. Unfortunately, despite all the good things experienced in Germany, there was a downside. While there, my mom and Dad had separated.

My mother sent me a letter sharing that they were getting a divorce. That broke my heart. I loved my dad so much. I cried for weeks. I prayed they would get back together but that did not happen. The thought of going back home became scary. I started to have trouble with my stomach again. So, I began to pray harder for me, and my family. I remember saying to my friend Lavern, *"There is always something to keep you praying."*

She said, *"Wait until you get married and have children. Praying is good and it makes you strong my friend."* I replied, *"I am beginning to think you are right Lavern."*

****

One day, as Lavern and I walked into the NCO club for lunch, we talked about the power of prayer and how sometimes God will make us wait.

When we got to our seat, she asked, "What is it that makes you so scared to trust people? What is the thing that has you looking like a deer in headlights?"

At that point, she took her mirror out of her purse and told me to look. I was surprised at what I saw. I was so sad. My eyes appeared so dark and there was no joy anywhere. That was another reason to pray. Everything always led back to praying and waiting for God to show up and fix whatever the "it" was at that time. There always seemed to be an "IT." I found myself praying for strength to share my painful story with this young woman, Lavern, who had taken me in as her little sister. I was 17 years old. She was married and had a 9-month-old baby boy who I often referred to as "my baby".

She asked, "How long is it going to take you to tell your story? I may not be able to fix it, but I can listen, and we can pray.

God said, *"where two or three are gathered, I am in the midst."*

As my eyes began to swell with tears, I started to tell my story. I shared the horrors of what I had experienced at 9, 10, and 11 years old and identified the person who inappropriately touched me for all those years. I felt so dirty and my violator had told me that I would be at fault if I told anyone. He went further by saying, "If your Father knew, he would leave your mom, and your mom would not be able to take care of five children by herself."

Because of all that he said, I didn't tell anyone.

I hated to see my father leave for work because that's when my violator would come to our home. He always found a way to get me by myself. As I look back, I often wondered how did that happen.

As I said that, Lavern said, *"If I weren't in Germany for the next 3 years, I would fly to Louisiana and help you tell your mom and Dad. I love you and I don't want you to have to go through that. Just know it is not your fault and you did nothing wrong. You are beautiful and wonderfully made."*

I went on to explain that this situation led to me having a relationship with God.

****

After receiving the news about my parents' separation and divorce, my family was no longer a family, and our home was no longer a home. Dad did not live with us anymore. Months later, Mom moved us to Baton Rouge, Louisiana and I became FREE from the pervert. I didn't have to face him anymore.

By time I saw him again, I was a grown woman with two daughters of my own.

I call on you, my God,
for you will answer me.
Turn your ear to me and hear my prayer.
Psalms 17:6

Chapter Five

My New Beginning

At 18 years of age, I left home to attended Southern University in Baton Rouge, the largest HBCU in Louisiana, on a full scholarship. I was excited to be a part of a college with a proud history and an excellent reputation. During those four years, I was free from all hurt, harm, and danger.

I must admit that amid the excitement I felt about this fresh start, I was a bit apprehensive as well. *Isn't it funny how you can be filled with two opposing thoughts at the same time about the same opportunity?* To do well in my academics was something instilled in me by my parents; as they were big on education. That was non-negotiable and very much a part of my acumen. What made me uncomfortable about my fresh start had to do with something else.

Growing up is inevitable but maturing as you grow is key. Being away from all that was familiar was the best choice for me. The promise that I made to myself is what carried me through, and I believe that many of the experiences while in college and the people placed in my path, were God's way of assisting me into my new journey to adulthood. I needed this unique environment more than I realized. I needed these new connections as well.

Two years prior to graduation from high school, three things shook me to my core which caused me to question myself and even the foundation I had been nurtured on. These isolated incidents not only shattered the confidence I had in those around me, specifically my family, but it caused me to lose trust in people. It caused me to question myself which proved to be very detrimental to my self-esteem.

****

As already shared, the sexual trauma and emotional trauma during my childhood, came about at the hands of close relatives. A cousin was the pedophile, and the other was the source of lies that caused me to miss my prom. These two circumstances had me question, why was I the easy target? Why did it seem that of all my siblings, to my knowledge, and my family found it welcoming to hurt me?

What I have not shared is that just before graduating high school, my aunt, while extremely angry about something, decided to tell me that the only father I knew; the one who raised me, provided for me, did his best to protect me and love me, was NOT my father. Can you imagine the shock and sense of betrayal? Time stood still. I was numb; speechless. As tears began to fall, I looked for an explanation from those who should have advocated for me, but no one had a rebuttable.

What do you mean he is not my father?

How is he not my father?

If he is not my real Dad, who is?

Once again, I became the victim of circumstances at the hands of a close family member. This time, however, it appeared that my mother and my father, or the man that I called my father, were also accomplices. Everyone knew, except for me. While my siblings and I shared the same mother, we didn't have the same father. What I also soon realized is that the teacher at my high school, who always favored me with special treats and gifts, was my aunt. She was my biological father's sister. That means she knew too. *Who else knew?*

Armed with this added information, I set out on a journey to not only meet my biological father but to build a relationship with him. I didn't weigh the fact that others may be uncomfortable with my mission. I didn't consider the feelings of others at all. I only wanted

• • •

to better understand who I was and how this happened. While genuine and innocent in my plight, I now realize how this campaign may have stirred up old wounds or even made some weary. Nevertheless, I pressed forward only to be hurt again.

My biological father didn't want to bond with me as I had hoped, and within the midst of this discovery, the father that raised me suffered a massive heart attack. And, in usual family fashion, I was told by my mother that his heart attack was my fault. More specifically, my decision to get to know my biological father caused his heart attack. Would I now go on in life with no father at all? One father has no desire to know me and the other one is faced with death.

Once again, my family attacked me. Once again, I was hurt and afraid. I didn't want to lose the only man I knew who loved me unconditionally the one I loved dearly. That night, I took my pain and fear to my bedroom. My whispers in the dark were simple, just as the angel Mary told me.

Dear God, I didn't mean to hurt my father, and I don't want to lose him. Please forgive me and heal him. In Jesus' name, Amen.

****

When I walked upon the campus of Southern University, I was armed with a commitment of academic excellence and with enthusiasm about my fresh start being a part of the Southern family. Being away from the source of all my childhood pain meant the promise of a new beginning for me. I was also armed with the belief that God was with me and for me and that when I whispered to Him, he would be waiting to hear me. What I was not armed with was the confidence I needed to be myself because I didn't know what that truly meant. Everything I thought I had been given in establishing my identity and sense of worth, had been pulled from under me by the very people I should have been able to trust. How do you start anew when you don't feel fully equipped?

Despite the trepidation that occasionally filled my head with thoughts, I began college with at least one commitment to myself; I to start college life as a virgin and to graduate as a virgin. This was my steadfast belief - "no sex before marriage." In addition to this, I remained committed to the values that I was taught as a child. Most days it was easy, other days were definitely challenging.

****

One challenge I faced was connecting with others and building relationships. At the onset, my roommates weren't friends with God, or at least their choices didn't seem as if they had a connection. They were always having a wonderful time and while I wanted to have a fun time with them, I just didn't know how. I wanted to fit in, but I also wanted to do what I believed was "right" for me. For example, socializing with them was always filled with good times and laughter. I met so many others on campus, which is good for building community, but the drinking and the smoking was too much.

When engaged in this activity, I immediately felt uncomfortable. Because I didn't always trust people, my mind would race with questions such as, what *would happen if I drank with them and became intoxicated? Who would look out for me? If I used drugs as my friends were known to do, how could I be sure that someone would not take advantage of me?* At the same, I had the opportunity to be around others who didn't engage in this type of extracurricular activity, but they were boring. I felt safe around them, but they didn't offer any element of fun. Most often, I chose fun despite the discomfort.

It wasn't long before my evenings were filled with card games and other co-ed social gatherings. My commitment to socializing resulted in my meeting many from everywhere. We shared stories about where we were from and our dreams and goals after graduation from college. Yes, the parties were often filled with activities that I did not approve of, but I didn't let that stop me from engaging in the entertainment. I remained true to my commitment of "no sex" and as previously shared drugs and alcohol were not my thing either.

Just as I was beginning to really enjoy my time at Southern, life brought about a need for change. This change warranted a choice that was influenced by my mother's response to my grades. They had dropped. My fun times of playing spades and hanging out in The Student Union had caught up with me.

My mother told me that I had two choices:

(1) bring up my grades or

(2) come home. I was on a full scholarship, so I chose to focus more on why I was there in the first place.

That was the best decision by far.

During the first year, I was introduced to the Dancing Dolls, Dancers who accompanied the marching band, The Human Juke Box, at every game. They were sharp, posed, and looked so confident during their performances. They had what I wanted. The truth is that my self-esteem was nonexistent and I lacked confidence; nevertheless, I tried out for the squad as soon as the first opportunity was presented.

The Band Director, was known by everyone on campus. He was like a bright light and every student including myself, loved him. There was never a time when he wasn't encouraging someone. He believed in the potential of his students as could always be found helping them in some way. Every time I saw him I made sure he knew that I loved being a part of the Southern family and that I admired the band. Being a part of the University gave me a sense of pride and belonging which I believe was key to being selected as a Dancing Doll.

Being a dancer meant practicing daily which was demanding and very exhausting. After practicing all summer, I was ready to quit because I found it hard to balance practice, attending classes, and time to complete my homework assignments. To say it was overwhelming is an understatement. When I communicated this with the Band Director, he assured me that I had worked too hard to quit. He encouraged me to hang on a little longer and not give in to the pressure. Our first performance was coming up and that would be my debut. He didn't want to see me cheat myself of that accomplishment. He further suggested that if I would stick it out, I could be considered as an alternate. He saw to it that I remained a part of the Dancing Dolls, which meant I was a part of a family, the Band Family. This also meant that I had the ear of the Band Director as a confidant and advisor. He looked out for me just as he was known for with many others on campus. Because of him, I felt more secure and confident in myself.

Another staff member who influenced my life was Mrs. J. When I shared my struggles with being a part of The Dancing Dolls, she immediately voiced her opinion. According to her, I didn't need to be a Doll. In her eyes, one didn't need to be "shaking their butt" to be a doll. She also added that I was a doll already and should consider something more sophisticated like becoming *Ms. Boley Hall.*

The title of *Ms. Boley Hall* was a prestigious one. To even run for this position, required you to meet certain educational standards, have a teacher/staff recommendation and a good reputation. My supporter was Mrs. J. She not only recommended me, but she guided and assisted me with every step of the campaign process. She assisted me with my promotional projects, coached me on how to prepare for debates, and when the dust settled, I was the last one standing out of fifteen applicants. To be crowned as *Ms. Boley Hall* meant a position of authority and leadership. I was not only responsible for my entire hall, but during Homecoming, I was a part of the Queen's Court. This meant that I would once again be on the field during the games but in a more sophisticated role. No shaking of the butt was required. To be crowned as *Ms. Boley Hall* boosted my confidence even more and it also placed me in a more influential position.

Whispers in the Dark

During my sophomore year, two prominent leaders in the African American Community, visited the campus. Their visit shifted my perspective of who I was as an asset to my community. I attended a rally that was being hosted by one of the leaders who was known as a great orator, but it was the female leader who made the biggest impression on me. I loved her hair, the clothes she wore, and how she carried herself. Her advocacy for women, especially Black women, was evident in her speech and was the biggest draw for me. To this day, I can recall what she said and from the first time I heard it, it became my life's mantra and one of the rules by which I chose to live my life.

When I consider my time at Southern, I am confident that it was one of the most impactful seasons of my life. It was in college that I made the conscious decision to be true to myself. I did this for myself and not because my parents told me to. No longer would I be afraid of the opinions of others or afraid to try new things. Because I stood for what was best for me, doors opened for me. The shift in my thinking allowed me to embrace the importance of the messaging I heard at the rally. If I had not experienced a shift in my mindset, I would not have been impressed by her words because fear would have kept me from even attending the rally. When I shifted my focus on what was best for me, I grew in confidence and my influence grew as well. Friends that I loved who weren't making good decisions, even changed because of my choices. They took school more seriously and began to embrace smart decisions.

There were many whispers in the dark during my time at Southern. I prayed to win card games for food money. I prayed to pass tests and to become a Dancing Doll. I prayed when Mrs. J pushed me outside of my comfort zone to run for *Ms. Boley Hall.* Just as in the past, I whispered in the dark because I knew that God would be waiting to listen.

When Mary the Angel came to visit me in the hospital many years before to assure me that God was waiting on me to talk to Him, I didn't doubt her, but I did ask God, "How do I know you are here?" Each time, I would always experience this fresh smell and air in my face that gave me peace to know He was with me. Once that happened, I would start talking.

He showed up night after night and year after year. I was so grateful for God's showing because when He did, I did not feel so alone My whispers and talks would always end in a peaceful night's rest.

Chapter Six

Marriage and Motherhood

I wish that I could say that I remained as faithful to God as He had been to me. There was a window of time when I found myself in a season of drought. During this time, there was not much whispering in the dark and I didn't attend church. It was also during this time that I felt like everything I loved had disconnected itself from me and I was living my life floundering. I still loved God, and I never lost faith in Him, but I was not serving Him. I considered this time in my life as my wilderness season.

Although my first two years at Southern served me well and helped to boost my confidence, I still had a void. I don't know if this attitude concerning life resurfaced before my former boyfriend came back into my life, or if it was because he came into my life. What I do know is that during this season, my attitude was "I don't care." I felt like I had lost everything that was near and dear to my heart. I had lost my family. I had lost my father because he had begun a new life with a new family. I had lost my church. What I did not know then is that this attitude and perspective stemmed from abandonment issues. So, while my confidence had been strengthened, I could not shake the fact that I had a deep fear of people leaving me. This fear resulted in me going above and beyond to make sure I did everything "right" so people would no longer leave me.

During my junior year of college, my boyfriend came home from the army and asked me to marry him. I said yes! He wasn't my first choice, but he was my best choice at the time. My fiancé' and I had been friends since childhood so there was truly little to tell him. He knew everything, including the fact that my childhood sweetheart and I were no longer connected. According to him, this was the motivation he needed to approach me. The fact that he knew me meant that he was familiar. He was a reminder of when things were good. Being with him did not require a lot of work. To say yes to him was easy.

My mom gave me the wedding that I had wanted all my life, and she did it alone. As beautiful as the wedding was, I had no father present to give me away. Looking back, I remember that I didn't whisper in the dark about this next step. I didn't whisper in the dark concerning anything else that pertained to my decision to get married, not even whether my boyfriend was the best choice for my life.

The first seven months of our marriage were great. We bought a home, and I began to decorate it as any woman would. This brought me so much joy and he knew it. While we couldn't have a honeymoon because I was still in college, that didn't matter to me because I was building a life in a new home with my husband. It was just me and him, doing everything together. We hosted our family at our home regularly. I didn't have a care in the world and my home was filled with fun and laughter; until I got pregnant.

I don't know if it was the pregnancy, the attention I was getting because we were pregnant, or something else that triggered him, but whatever it was things changed fast. At month seven of our marriage, we found out that I was pregnant. This was a God-sent gift. I was having a baby and we both were happy about it. Unfortunately, I was sick for the entire nine months and I didn't want to do anything after coming home from classes. In the fourth month of my pregnancy, he snapped, and I began to take a lot of physical, mental, and verbal abuse from him. To describe the occurrences as traumatic would be accurate. The cause behind the abuse and the fact that I was living it was traumatic. This trauma was nothing I was prepared for and was not the dream I had when I thought of married life. To be amid, what I would call a nightmare was not good and not something I wanted my child to be exposed to. The full realization of my circumstances caused me to take things more seriously. I had to get out.

To find out that I was pregnant with my baby girl was a gift from God. It was once said that I may never have children, but once again God defied the odds. I prayed for a healthy baby and that's exactly what He gave me. God knew that I wanted to be a parent and despite my complacency, He answered my prayer, and I was determined to do what I could to protect this gift. I did not want my child raised in a home full of pain, anger, and fear. I had experienced enough of that for everyone.

My husband had issues from his time in the army. I won't go into the particulars of that because that is his story to tell. What I will say is that I did not want my daughter exposed to the lifestyle I had managed to suffer through. When she was three months old, I made my first attempt to leave. Unfortunately, this attempt proved unsuccessful as even the police sided with my husband concerning paternity rights. Even though I was leaving because of the fear for my safety, the authorities focused more on the fact that I was taking my husband's child. I was told that it was illegal for me to take his child.

So, I stayed and prayed to God for guidance. Even as conditions got worse, I continued to pray. I was grateful for my beautiful home and a healthy child, but I had a husband from hell due to his PTSD and his refusal to accept help. The answer to my situation, per my prayers to God, was to read my Bible for all my answers and just wait.

I found solace in reading the Bible. The scriptures gave me strength and strategy. My prayers and commitment to reading scripture brought me closer to God. This strength fostered the spirit of perseverance that I needed when the authorities (police) would not help me. It fueled my spirit and with the help of my parents, I had a grand plan.

In another attempt to leave my husband, to leave the danger, I called my family from a pay phone. I had escaped and needed them to pick me up. Because of Louisiana Law, they could not come to our home to get me because they would be breaking the law. To remove me from my husband's home was not the best option, but the phone booth worked fine.

Trusting and believing in God was the key to my victory. God provided the foundation on which I stood when I defied the odds. I can remember like it was yesterday. I woke up and heard His voice. He said it was time. I had one more year of college to complete, but I did not care. His voice said move, and I did just that. I packed clothing for my daughter and myself and wrote a long letter to my husband explaining how I felt and why I believed the things in our life were all wrong. I was picked up from the phone booth and taken to the airport. I took my daughter to Fayetteville, North Carolina so that she and I could be safe. My mother's brother, my uncle whom I had visited in Germany years before, opened his home to me and my baby girl. Nobody knew where we were, but for at least 6 months we were safe. Even if I had taken my child away from my husband, which was against the law, I was in a place where trauma did not greet me or greet us every day.

When my daughter was 9 months old, I returned to Baton Rouge to finish school. I moved in with my aunt, my mother's sister. I began working at Kmart, returned to school to finish my degree, and did what it took to care for myself and my beautiful daughter. After my daughter turned 3 years old, I met a man who brought me joy, and after a while, I found myself pregnant with my second daughter. While it may not have been the perfect situation, I was extremely happy and thankful that God had blessed me with another beautiful daughter. I was excited. My oldest daughter was excited to be a big sister. Things were good.

I never wanted to remarry, but I did want to raise my daughters "the right way." My decision to not remarry stemmed from my fear of being abused. I refused to have my girls exposed to that lifestyle. In addition to this, I would not allow anyone to claim legal rights to take my children away from me. When my relationship ended due to infidelity, my girls and I moved to Memphis, Tennessee. Now being a single parent, I was even more determined to keep my girls safe and to raise them the right way. I asked God for wisdom so that I may please Him in this formidable responsibility of mothering.

Life with my girls consisted of daily talks, evening meals, and nightly prayers. I made sure they were active in the church. Because of what I experienced as a child, I made no assumptions concerning their safety or being exposed to things they should not have been. I would always ask them how they were doing. I would ask if anyone, family, or friends, made them uncomfortable or touched them inappropriately. I was transparent with my girls and shared with them my experience of sexual assault. I gave them specific instructions on what to do if they were in danger. I often conveyed and reminded them of their value to me and how much of a blessing they were to me.

They were my gifts from God, and I made sure they were comfortable to talk with me about anything. We talked about what it meant to honor God in our lives, and the importance of honesty, loyalty, commitment, and faithfulness. I taught them to show kindness to people, what it meant to be respectful, and how to carry themselves like a lady. Open conversation, love, and laughter filled our home. For that, I was truly thankful.

****

Due to a change in my sister's household dynamics, I had custody of my niece and nephew for about five years. Just as I did my best to care for my daughters, I extended the same love and care to my niece and nephew. They were mine and I was their "Auntie Mama." Collectively, they all had a great life filled with activities and opportunities. I worked hard to provide for them. Two jobs and a cleaning business were once a part of my reality, and I did it all for them. Whether it was summer camps, band camp, cheer camp, beta club, or football, they had what they needed. Child support was nonexistent, so I had to make it happen. As already proven by my life, years before, I could not always depend on "family" to show up, so by God's grace, I did the best I could for the kids. And, in all my doing for them, I taught them the importance of working for what they want as well. They often joined me in the cleaning jobs. It was a family affair.

As they grew, I asked God for guidance to make the best decisions and to protect my children from seen and unseen dangers, especially from perverts. I prayed for their health, peace, and their joy. Even before my girls married, I prayed for their future husbands. While they were young, I taught them to pray and shared the importance of "Whispering in the Dark" and having a relationship with God. Thankfully, my children grew to be very respectful, humble, and thankful. Even today, I am blessed to say my children (all four of them) are my greatest joy. When I think of the years I had raising them, I whisper, *"Thank you Father for allowing me to be their mom. I pray that I made you proud."*

Chapter Seven

The Veil is Lifted

All the years I spent whispering in the dark, I didn't know God was preparing me for the call He had on my life. As a young girl, the mothers of our church would always tell me that I had a "veil over my face." I never knew what that meant. It sounded like it was something special, but I could not see it or understand it.

Despite all my failings, shortcomings, and wrong decisions, I always wanted to know and understand God's Word. As I matured, I returned to my times with Him in the dark and the sense of peace that I felt with every conversation. After raising my children, I decided to take my desire to know more to another level, so I went to theology school. My concentration on biblical studies fulfilled my desire to know more. Little did I know that upon completion my Pastor would commission me to the assignment of Pastor over the Seniors Connect Group of our church.

I am gifted with a passion for teaching and encouraging others, which I have engaged in for over 42 years. This has always come easy for me. Now, because of the assignment entrusted to me by my Pastor, I can couple my passions of teaching and knowing more about God into one place, as the leader of a group of phenomenal people, aged fifty and up. Even now, 11 years later, I remain committed to the assignment.

Working with children in a classroom setting prepared me. The prayers prayed when attempting to reach a child, understand a child, help a child, and even get through the various stressors associated with education were the perfect preparation ground for my next. Keeping

God at the forefront of it all was the key to my being able to achieve success and make an impact. My relationship with Him, in addition to "staying on my Ps" - *Prayer, Priorities, Peace, Positivity, Patience, and Perseverance* - was the recipe. In addition to this, I was committed to giving. What you plant into the lives of others will always come back. It was this life's philosophy that served as the foundation for my decision to always give my tithes, use my talents, and share my time with others, especially those things that serve to build up God's people. Every pay period translated into paying my tithes, giving, and blessing another financially. Every week for 11 years, I used my talent and gave my time to the Senior Connect Group at no charge. In addition to this, I served and made sacrifices toward educating our youth.

When assigned to my ministry group, I noticed a few things that I needed to address immediately before I could truly make an impact. The three areas in which I chose to focus were (a) building their trust, (b) building their confidence, and (c) building a community.

In building their trust, I often shared with my team that we were in this thing together. I wanted them to know that we were there for each other, to support each other, and to learn from each other. This included me. I always emphasized that my number one objective was to make sure God was pleased with us both individually and collectively and that we would be accountable to each other and would create a safe place to share, laugh, cry, and celebrate.

In building their confidence, I encouraged their participation in our events and meetings. Many of them seemed to be shy, but I soon found out that they were quiet because they could not read well, or didn't feel as if they had anything to contribute. By creating opportunities to read scriptures aloud, pray aloud, and even share their testimonies during our special occasions, I fostered environments that served to boost their confidence. Over time, they no longer shied away from being heard or from volunteering.

Whispers in the Dark

Many of those within my ministry group are widowed, lived alone, and had no other social interaction outside of church. I knew that creating a community was important. When any of my members are ill or unable to attend services, my face would be one of the first they would see. Another member would accompany me as we visited with them, prayed with them, administered communion, and even helped with small tasks. I implemented the concept of prayer partners within the group as well. This was my way of ensuring that everyone had someone always looking out for them. In addition to the ministerial assignments, I created a quarterly social that would give everyone a reason to get dressed up and "let their hair down." During these quarterly events, we would have a guest speaker to share on topics relevant to the group. These quarterly events and yearly trips, such as a visit to the diamond mine and a cruise to Mexico, served as our time to rest, relax, and relate. My connect group has been described as one of the strongest in our church. To that I always reply, "To God be the Glory!"

Serving in ministry is one of my life's joys and I am thankful that my Pastor afforded me the opportunity. The Mothers in my church decades before said that God would use me. Even their reference to the veil came back to the forefront when my Senior Pastor officially commissioned me as a Pastor of my group.

During my confirmation, he said, "Now you can come from behind the veil."

The veil is a place of comfort and protection. Spiritually, it signifies a place of isolation and a means by which one has been set apart. This is what the mothers were saying all along.

It has been eleven wonderful years since being assigned to the Seniors Connect Group. We have laughed, cried, grown closer, and most importantly, become stronger together in the things of God. To be assigned this responsibility has been a blessing for both them and me. This journey has been one of great faith and whispering in the dark more than ever as there was always an occasion to speak with God.

When one accepts a call or assignment to lead, it does not preclude trials of their own. Even while battling life's circumstances, leaders continue to show up and remain committed to their assignment. As with other leaders in position, I continued to serve my Seniors Connect Group when trials, heartbreak, and the fight for my life were my reality.

In February 2022, my best friend died. I was devastated. Her death was a hard pill to swallow and at any given time, I would find myself full of tears. Grieving privately and showing up for others publicly was challenging but I found a way to push through. Just when I began to gather my footing, my sister, my children's father, my bonus daughter, and my bonus granddaughter died in November 2022. That's five close friends and family members. Five deaths in one year; I was an emotional wreck, but I continued to pour into the group. I continued to plan our events and worked to ensure our community remained connected.

During life's challenges, God afforded me the strength to endure. As I whispered in the dark for others, I whispered for myself as well. I faced my biggest personal battle: a breast cancer diagnosis on September 7, 2022 which came with a double mastectomy on November 1st in the same year. All of this happened while grieving all of those who I loved. I pressed through by the grace of God and in looking back, I know that I am stronger and better. My commitment to whisper in the dark is the key to it all.

Chapter Eight

Loving My Authentic Self

It has been over five decades since I was first sexually assaulted by a cousin, which I endured for about five years. This experience was the precursor to losing trust in people. This trauma took away my innocence and replaced it with a life filled with fear and anxiety at an early age.

It has been the same amount of time since the relationship with my maternal aunt was damaged. It was within this same year that I was told that my father, the man who had been in my life all my life, was not my father. My trust and sense of stability were attacked, which reinforced the belief that my family treated me differently from all the others. Why did it seem as if everyone hated me or wanted to hurt me?

Can you imagine what it must be like to live in a world that no longer made sense? Where did I belong? To whom did I truly belong? Who loved me? Why were my family members, those that I should be able to rely upon, attacking me, and treating me with such disdain? What started as a child continued throughout my life. Why did my father, my first love, abandon me? Why did my biological father not want to have anything to do with me? Or so I thought as a youngster.

Can you imagine how all this negatively affected me as a child and served to create a narrative in my head about relationships with others? I would overthink everything. I pushed to do "and then some" because I wanted to be accepted. I felt as though I had to go above and beyond, to be loved and appreciated. Maybe if I went the extra mile or pushed to excel in everything, I would be acknowledged, valued, and not be pushed away or abandoned. Then I would be at peace in my skin; peace is something that I had not felt in years.

The Word of God tells us that He will give us *"beauty for ashes"* and that *"all things work together for good."* How could one truly find good or beauty in what I have experienced? Only God could make that possible. His promise for me never changed and each time I whispered in the dark, deposits were made that would serve to secure my future.

I am no longer the timid little girl, but rather a woman who stands bold.

I am no longer the one with low self-esteem and confidence. I am self-aware and confident in the fact that I am God's masterpiece, His unique creation.

I no longer live in fear. Although I face challenges and uncertainties, I tackle each with the courage that God has instilled in me by way of his Holy Spirit.

I was once a people pleaser. It was my strategy to gain attention and love others. Now, I know that being accepted by Christ is all that I need. I no longer feel as though I don't belong. The community that God gave me and the one I created for myself is all I need.

One of the biggest blessings that came to me was the visit from Nurse Mary, my angel. She was the one who encouraged me to pray. She gave me the tools needed to overcome all my challenges and fears. While I did not know it at the time, her reassurance that God wanted to hear from me, is what served to shift the trajectory of my life. *Whispering in the Dark* was one of the keys that served to unlock the doors for the "beauty" and the "good" that I now enjoy. Even amid life's challenges, my life is filled with God's beauty. I now have true freedom. I have true peace.

The Lord will fight for you;
you need only to be still.
Exodus 14:14

Letter From a Friend

What can I say about Terri Lane Jackson-Hunt? Well, here is our story, I met Terri through a former Head Start co-worker. We hit it off and we have known each other for over 40+ years. We spent more time packing our 6 children up with us in a 5.0 Mustang traveling to Baton Rouge every weekend to fellowship with her family which I claim as "MY Family". My baby boy was in her wedding.

Terri and I have travelled up and down Highway 55 on numerous occasions. Sometime for sad occasions, but overall to celebrate every occasion especially Mardi Gras and just enjoying time with her sisters, especially Mary Ann who is no longer with us.

We have a special bond in which we don't have to call each other every day but we have a sixth sense to know when something is good or bad. "Girl what's wrong?" or I can look at her eyes and know when something is not going like it should, "What's up Terri?" and we began to share.

Terri also knows she has to share her Momma and Sisters, with me. I appreciated it when she spoke at my son's funeral. That gave me so much comfort. I know she knew more about him than the pastor. I want to take this time to honor you, tell you congratulations and how proud I am of you and all your achievements. Always remember you are an overcomer and a survivor.

You have always reminded me to keep God first and trust him no matter what. You are so full of wisdom; you are a classic lady and full of integrity. I am blessed to know you and call you friend.

Love you my sister in Christ,

Mary Ferguson Calhoun

My fellow believers, when it seems as though you are facing nothing but difficulties, see it as an invaluable opportunity to experience the greatest joy that you can! For you know that when your faith is tested, it stirs up in you the power of endurance. And then as your endurance grows stronger, it will release perfection into every part of your being until there is nothing missing and nothing lacking.
James 1:2-4 TPT

Gratitude of a Friend

In the Bible and throughout history, there are women who have shared their truth and been authentic about their journey as they paved the way for generational healing in a complex and complicated society. Dr. Terri Lane Hunt is one of those remarkable women to which the world will forever be indebted for her ability to nurture, love, and edify those who cross her path. This profound storyteller is genuine and purposeful as she draws the individual into a most heart wrenching experience while providing nuggets of power and wisdom from which to draw strength and encouragement.

I have had the privilege to sit at her feet to grow in wisdom and understanding. Dr. Terri Lane Hunt is unafraid to bare the gospel, connecting it to her actual lived experiences. Her words speak life, restore lives, and encourages others. This phenomenal woman of God is bringing a taboo topic into the light to not only heal herself yet many of countless women and girls who are still Whispering in the Dark.

I extend the deepest gratitude to Dr. Terri Lane Hunt for allowing our Father to use her as a restoration vessel for years to come.

Deadre Ussery,
Former Executive Director,
Schools of Perea and Beloved Friend

And we all, with unveiled face, continually seeing as in a mirror the glory of the Lord, are progressively being transformed into His image from [one degree of] glory to [even more] glory, which comes from the Lord, [who is] the Spirit.

2 Corinthians 3: 18 AMP

About the Author

Terri Lane Jackson (Dr. Terri Hunt) was born in New Orleans Louisiana, raised in St. Gabriel Louisiana, and after several moves during her formative and adult years makes her home in Memphis, Tennessee. She enjoys music, shopping, reading, cooking, and traveling overseas in her spare time. After 20 years of teaching at the schools of Perea and 10 years at schools for the military, Dr. Hunt has now dedicated her life to working in the Kingdom of God teaching seniors at New Direction Christian Church. Whether serving as a teacher, a tutor, or a mentor to the young men and women at the schools of Perea and New Direction Christian Church, Dr. Terri is committed to serving others.

Made in the USA
Columbia, SC
05 November 2024

45429422R00035